I Forgive You

Written by Judy Billing
Illustrated by Olha Tkachenko

To my darling, precious Mama!
For anytime I let you down,
Caused a tear or made you frown
... forgive me.

I FORGIVE YOU
Billing, Judy - author, 2018
Illustrations, layout & design by Olha Tkachenko, Little Big Me Publishing, 2019
WWW.LITTLEBIG.ME
ISBN: 978-1-7751079-8-9
All rights © Judy Billing. No part of this publication may be reproduced, stored
in retrieval system, or transmitted in any form or by any means: electronic, mechanical,
photocopying, recording, or otherwise, without the prior written permission of the author.

Why must I forgive the
boy who was bad?
He took all my toys and
made me feel sad.
He thought he was funny
when he made me cry.
Why must I forgive him?
I need to know why.

Grandma says that it's simple, as simple can be.
I must forgive him because God forgives me.

Why must I forgive my big sister, a teen?
She always torments me and treats me so mean.
When I ask why she does it, she says, "Just because."
Why must I forgive the mean things that she does?

Grandma says that it's simple, as simple can be. I must forgive her because God forgives me.

Why must I forgive my neighbour next door?
He yells when I walk past. He makes it a chore.
I go past his house when I walk down my street.
He's the grumpiest person that you'll ever meet!

Grandma says that it's simple, as simple can be.
I must forgive him because God forgives me.

Why must I forgive when I'm winning the game,
And my friends get upset and they call me a name?
It doesn't seem fair and it doesn't seem right.
Why must I forgive them when they start the fight?

Grandma says that it's simple, as simple can be.
I must forgive them because God forgives me.

Why must I forgive when my brother's a pest?
He tries to annoy me when I want to rest.
I won't understand this, as long as I live.
When others are mean, why must I forgive?

Grandma says that it's simple, as simple can be.
I must forgive him because God forgives me.

There are so many bullies; they make me so mad.
I don't want to like them; they're mean and they're bad.
They always hurt others without thinking twice.
Why must I forgive them and still treat them nice?

Grandma says that it's simple, as simple can be.
I must forgive them because God forgives me.

And then I remember some things that I've done,
Some things that were not nice, which I thought were fun.
When I talked to my Grandma, she said, "God loves you.
Tell God that you're sorry - but you must mean it, too."

I remember that one day I said a bad word.
And it was the baddest word I'd ever heard!
At times I was cranky and I don't know why,
But I acted so naughty and made my mom cry.

I asked God's forgiveness, to which He replied,
"Yes, I forgive you; that's why Jesus died."

One day during lunch, when I spilled my drink,
I lied when I said, "It was my brother, I think."
I got him in trouble and then I felt bad
Because it was my fault my brother was sad.

I asked God's forgiveness, to which He replied, "Yes, I forgive you; that's why Jesus died."

And one day, I took my kid sister's doll.
I hid it in the closet that's in our front hall.
I didn't want to hurt her; I was just having fun,
But her eyes filled with tears and they started to run.

God, thank You for teaching me, I must forgive,
As long as I'm breathing, as long as I live.
For no one is perfect, no one except You.
I love You, dear Jesus, for all that You do.

I thank You, dear Father, for sending Your Son.
I thank You, dear Jesus, for being the One
Who died on the Cross so that I could be free.
I will forgive others because you forgive me.

Amen!

www.ingramcontent.com/pod-product-compliance
Lightning Source LLC
Chambersburg PA
CBHW051304110526
44589CB00025B/2938